RED,
CHERRY
RED

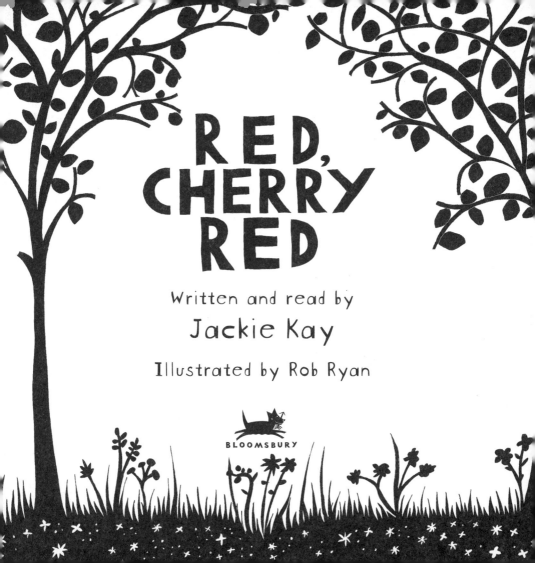

RED, CHERRY RED

Written and read by
Jackie Kay

Illustrated by Rob Ryan

BLOOMSBURY

First published in Great Britain in 2007 by Bloomsbury Publishing Plc
36 Soho Square, London, W1D 3QY

Text copyright © Jackie Kay 2007
Illustrations copyright © Rob Ryan 2007

Audio CD produced by Jill Waters and recorded at The Audio Workshop
Read by Jackie Kay
'The Moon at Knowle Hill' music
composed, performed and copyright © Hugh Nankivell 2007

The moral rights of the author and illustrator have been asserted

A CIP catalogue record of this book is available from the British Library

ISBN 978 0 7475 8979 2

The paper this book is printed on is certified by the © 1996 Forest
Stewardship Council A. C. (FSC). It is ancient-forest friendly. The
printer holds FSC chain of custody SGS-COC-2939

FSC

Mixed Sources
Product group from well-managed
forests and other controlled sources

Cert no. SGS-COC-2939
www.fsc.org
© 1996 Forest Stewardship Council

Typeset by Dorchester Typesetting Group Ltd
Printed and bound in Italy by L.E.G.O.

1 3 5 7 9 10 8 6 4 2

www.bloomsbury.com/jackiekay

For Matthew,
my rock,
with love

Contents

MY FACE IS A MAP

I was born with a map of Australia on my face;
it was beautiful, my mother told me –
there was nobody like me in the whole wide world
who could trace the edges of down under
on the raised and grafted song lines of her face.

I was connected to the upside-down people,
to those who loved the bush and the kangaroo.
I could never smile or frown or weep
in case my special map fell off my face.
My face was pulled tight, so that nobody got lost.

I held my head steady and I held my head high.
When people gaped and gawped and gawked
I thought they were trying to find Alice Springs,
to work out where they wanted to go, where they'd been.
And when somebody stared for a very long time

I would simply ask if they'd been down under:
the hardest human heart melts when it sees a koala bear.
My words were slower than other children's
because my map was stitched to my mouth:
every time I managed a whole sentence

I imagined a small boat floating out of Sydney harbour.
Yesterday there was talk of peeling my map off,
changing my face, so that it looks like others;
my mother said I should have a long think,
and that maybe life would be easier . . .

I am thinking now, staring hard into the mirror.
I trace the hard edges of the world in my face.
I know the hard stares of some people.
Without my map, will I be the same person?
Will I know where I am, where I have been?

YELL SOUND

I always looked out at the world
and wondered if the world looked back at me,
standing on the edge of something –
on my face the wind from the cold sea.

Across the waters were mirrors to see
faces that looked like me,
people caught between two places,
people crossing over the seas.

And it seemed from my croft
– with the old stones and the sheep,
and the sound of the songs in my sleep –
that the music of folk somewhere meets

on the edge of the place we would be.
I've lived through some hard times.
My face is lined; my body so frail.
I used to think I might be able –

when the river ran to meet the sea,
when the sun and moon shared the sky –
to look out as far as the eye could see,
and raise a glass to the girl looking back at me.

MRS DUNGEON BRAE

Mrs Dungeon Brae lived on the Isle of Mull,
the fairest of the rarest
of all the western isles,
in a ramshackle farm house,
close to the hoarse, heaving sea.

Every morning Mrs Dungeon Brae
was up with her white goats,
pulling their teats for thin milk.
If she stumbled across a stranger
on her acre of land,

she reached for her gun – an old
long gun that belonged to her father,
his father before him, his father before him –
then fired in the fern-scented air
and watched the crows and strangers scatter.

She laughed a grim dry cough of a laugh.
Her face had all of Scotland's misery,
every battle fought and lost;
but her cheeks were surprises – a dash
of colour, a sprig of purple heather

peeping over the barren hillside.
Then, alone in her house,
she sat down in her armchair,
with her grey hair yanked into a bun,
and died –

a tight, round ball of a death
– and nobody has found her.
Everybody is terrified of trespassing.
So the skeleton of Mrs Dungeon Brae
sits on her favoured armchair,

and the radio is playing Bach.

Ach. Ach.

Mrs Dungeon Brae.

The strings haunting the bones of Mrs Dungeon Brae.

Ach. Ach. Mrs Dungeon Brae. Ach. Ach.

THE KNITTER

I knit to keep death away,
for hame will dae me.
On a day like this the fine mist
is a dropped stitch across the sky.

I knit to hold a good yarn,
for stories bide with me
on a night like this, by the peat fire;
I like a story with a herringbone twist.

But a yarn aye slips through your fingers.
And my small heart has shrunk with years.
I can't measure the gravits, the gloves, the mittens,
the jerseys, the cuffs, the hose, the caps,

the cowls, the cravats, the cardigans,
the hems and facings over the years.
Beyond the sea wall the waves unfurl.
I have knitted through the wee stitched hours.

I have knitted till my eyes filled with tears,
till the dark sky filled with colour.
Every spare moment. Time is a ball of wool.
I knit to keep my croft; knit to save my life.

When my man was out at sea I knitted the fishbone.
Three to the door, three to the fire.
The more I could knit, the more we could eat.
I knitted to mend my broken heart

when the sea took my man away, and by day
I knitted to keep the memories at bay.
I knitted my borders by the light of the fire
when the full moon in the sky was a fresh ball of yarn.

I knitted to begin again: lay on, sweerie geng.
Takkin my makkin everywhere I gang.
Een and een. Twin pins. My good head.
A whole life of casting on, casting off,

like the North Sea. I watch wave after wave,
plain and purl, casting on, casting off.
I watch the ferries coming back, going away.
Time is a loop stitch. I knit to keep death away.

WOMAN GUTTING HERRING

There's my hands,
and there's the herring,
and there's me pulling the innards oot,
day in day oot.
Sometimes my hands look like the herring
and sometimes the herring look like my hands:
slippery silver fish.

I have my scarf on over my head,
and my head leans over the trough of fish,
and my back is bent like a fish,
all the long day.
And when I get home I wash and wash my hands,
but I can never get the smell to go away.
Sometimes I dream they have all come to life
and are swimming away – silver fishes.

THE FISHERMAN

No matter how the north-westerly wind blows
on a day like this, no matter how bad the weather,
the old man remembers the storms of the past better:

the winters when the snow stayed for an age,
the wind at his bedroom window on the rampage,
the sea like some great beast loose from its cage.

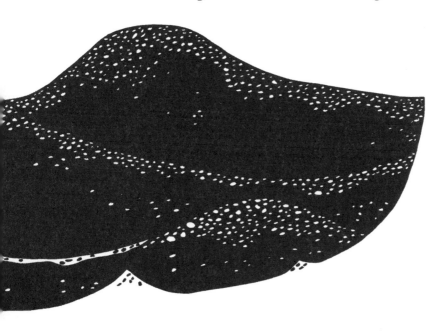

Remembers the cut of cliffs, steaming with spray,
the sea roaring as if it had something to say,
that small boat, clear as anything; his first day.

And the way the sea lifted them up and threw them down.
The way the old men talked of getting sea legs,
the way the sea was feared like God Almighty.

Remembers the wild heaving, the curses and swearing,
and the flashes of men between the frantic spraying;
every trip home you were glad of surviving.

The past is all waves for the fisherman now.
The past is boats and waves and nets –
what you lost and what you found,

the wild rough days, then the sudden, surprising
moments of calm, like thaw melting the snow,
like the heart melting after a row.

'Yes, yes.' The old man stares out of his window.
'Old friend and enemy,' he addresses the sea,
'by Christ, you gave me a rough ride for my money.'

The fisherman rubs his stubbly chin.
'Yes, well, that was back then in the lucid days.
Now, now, it is time to get ready for spring.'

THE ANGLER'S SONG

Down where I am, my love, there is no love.
There is no light, no break of day, no rising sun.
Where I am, I call you in; I open my large mouth.
The only light down here comes from my body.

Down where I am is deeper than you imagine.
There is no food, no easy prey, and it is freezing cold.
I sing to make you say my name. My big eyes weep.
This is the world of never-ending darkness, like pain.

Come down. I have been waiting for you a long time.
I wait without appearing to wait.
I see without being seen to see. You know me.
I am big-headed. I am hideous. I am ugly.

Come down. When I find you, I will bite into your belly.
What you see is what you get with me.
There is no other way. I will become you, let us say.
All that will be left of me will be my breathing.

Come down where I am. In and out, out and in.
Down at the very bottom of the deep dark sea.
When I become you, my mouth will stay open.
My open mouth like the river mouth down at the bottom.

Come down where I am. I will flash my lights for you.
My large eyes will take you in, contain you.
I make no promises. I offer nothing. Not even light.
Down, deep down in the dark, at the bottom, is my bed.

My sea bed, love, where there are no promises of love.
Dark – where there are no promises of light.
Where there is little hope of food.
Where day and night are night and day.

My sea bed. I tell no lies so your heart
will not be broken. I offer nothing.
All you will have is my breathing.
But I will give myself up to you.

I will give myself up for you.

LEAVING HOME

On the night that I was leaving
the old waves were high;
I lay small inside the dark
as the waves tore me apart.

On the night that I was leaving
I was strewn around the cabin;
my body belonged to the boat
as the waves tore me apart

on the night that I was leaving
to try and make a new start.
I felt sick to my stomach
as the waves tore me apart

on the night that I was leaving.
The wind battered at the boat;
I tried to still my broken heart
as the waves tore me apart.

MY GRANDMOTHER'S PINK RIVER

My grandmother's river knitted plain and purl,
rows of pink, never dropped a stitch,

never cast off, kept on and on, a big ball
of pink wool, the colour of poached salmon.

My grandmother's river woke early in the morning
and stayed awake most of the night,

tossing and turning and twitching in her dreams,
clicking her teeth, sucking her old soggy gums.

My grandmother's river collected things
– saucepans, tyres, handbags, wellingtons –

and hid them in her bottom drawer
with the river bass and river chub and river crab,

the brown stones, grey stones and green plants,
the brown trout, perch, pike and wishing coins.

My grandmother's river kneaded dough, pounded butter,
melted all over the riverbanks years and years later

when the sluice gates opened and the river rose
and sloshed and spilled over the fields.

My grandmother's river wept in the end:
flooded the banks, floated the houses like boats.

My grandmother's river's cry that dark lost night
was a long babbling, burbling, bubbling into the sea.

AN OLD WOMAN'S FIRE

I remember watching my grandmother build her fire,
the honest kindling, the twisted newspaper,
the tiny tower of good black coal.
And how, once lit, she'd hold a sheet of newspaper
across the fire and say, 'Watch it suck, dear.'

I remember the way my grandmother loved to poke her fire –
always nudging the coals and turning them over,
opening the grate, placing another jet jewel on the glowing fire –
and how she'd fuss over the dying embers.

I remember how she sat there in her armchair,
her old face a little pink and flushed from the heat.
And how she'd smile at her coal fire lovingly,
and sigh, 'There's nothing like a real fire, is there, dear?'

As if her life could have been something else entirely.

BUSH FIRE

That fire, they said, was red as red as red
as red as a fox, your lips, a cherry;
that fire, they said, spread and spread and spread,
faster than a cheetah or a nasty rumour;
that fire, they said, was hot, so hot, so hot,
hotter than lava or an African summer.

That fire, they said, was angry, very angry.
For three roaring days, it danced wildly, wildly, wildly.
Wild as flamenco, strip the willow, a Highland fling.
That fire, they said, had a big bad mouth,
swearing, spluttering, 'Bring it on! Bring it on!'

That fire, they said, wolfed down the lot –
the lovely little homes, the trees, the land.
That fire, they said, left nothing behind at all:
one blackened trail, one sad scorched story.

AUNT PEGGY

Aunt Peggy's wings were clipped last May.
She sleeps with her small feet stuck out,
her head tucked under her shoulder.

Aunt Peggy squawks and complains:
the price of food, her bills, the electric.
She flaps about when the phone rings.

Aunt Peggy listens with her head to the side.
She stays away from the window.
She pulls her curtains tight at night.

Aunt Peggy says, 'It's an absolute disgrace.'
She stands on one leg, shifts to the other.
'Nothing much ever happens any more.'

NO. 115 DREAMS

The living room remembers Gran dancing to Count Basie.
The kitchen can still hear my aunts fighting on Christmas Day.
The hall is worried about the loose banister.
The small room is troubled by the missing hamster.
The toilet particularly dislikes my grandfather.
The wallpaper covers up for the whole family.

And No. 115 dreams of lovely houses by the sea.
And No. 115 dreams of one night in the country.

The stairs are keeping schtum about the broken window.
The toilet's sick of the trapped pipes squealing so.
The walls aren't thick enough for all the screaming.
My parent's bedroom has a bed in a choppy sea.
My own bedroom loves the bones of me.
My brother's bedroom needs a different boy.

And No. 115 dreams of yellow light, an attic room.
And No. 115 dreams of a chimney, a new red roof.

And the red roof dreams of robin redbreasts
tap-dancing on the red dance floor in the open air.

RED RUNNING SHOES

I wore some other girl's red running shoes
with real spikes like rose thorns under my foot.

I got into position: my limbs seriously tense,
one knee on the asphalt, one foot flat, all that.

I crouched over, hands down, like a predator
ready for prey; and took off, took flight

on the red running track, so fast I could be fear
running, a live fright, a chance vision.

My dark hair wild in the wind.
My arms pounding light years, thin air, euphoria.

I flew past in some other girl's red running shoes,
round the red track near the railway line.

I raced straight towards the future.
The past was left standing behind, waving.

I ran and ran; my feet became the land.
I couldn't tell if the ground was moving under my feet,

shifting sand, or if I might ever just stop, like a heartbeat.
It felt as if I would run for ever, hard pounding feet,

until I ran right into myself, years on,
sat still, heavy, past forty, groaning, the streak lightning gone.

HAUF A DOZEN

My maw telt me tae buy:
hauf a dozen eggs,
a big bag o' tatties,
a loaf o' bread, an a tin o' beans,
an tae check ma change
an I wuid get sixpence.

Ma maw said tae mind
an see that the none o' the eggs
were cracked awready;
tae hurry back hame
tae ma mammy or I wuid
get six o' her best.

Well. I forgot the bread.
You'd forget your head if it wisnae screwed on.
I didnae look in at the eggs,
lift each wan gently an check
its bottom. My maw's haund wis itchin.
Wan o' the hauf dozen eggs wis caved in,

smashed up like Humpty Dumpty.
Ave no got a guid memory.
I'm aye at sixes and sevens.
I'm scatty like a chicken.
An till that day I didnae ken
that six wis hauf a dozen.

SKETCH OF GIRL IN CLASS

Her eyes are opals, milky, loving,
or a pool her younger self might have swam in.
There is yesterday in one eye,
the day before in the other.
Maybe she looks like her grandmother.
She's thinking about her dogs,
howling behind her front door,
and her mother's constant pain in the side.
Her two hands almost meet,
thumb to worried thumb.
She holds a blue pen in her left hand.
She's frightened of people laughing
behind her back.
On her back she wears a blue blazer.
She fears the long still night.
Her shoes are black, weather-worn.
Her feet rest firm on the ground

of the big classroom.
She dreams of wild animals
running darkly across the moors.
She wears black tights on her plump legs.
Just now, her hand touched her face
as if for a moment
she'd forgotten who she was.

RIVER REFLECTION

Standing by the river, my face grew
into a flat fish and floated off
to a lily pad, and I was lonely
without myself, without my twin.

The river kept going on and on,
talking to itself dark thoughts,
and the rain started pattering on my face,
so that I looked like a spotted leaf.

And my eyes searched the river for my past
that might lie thick and slow underneath –
until somebody called my name,
and I walked home, turning my back on myself.

STICK INSECT

My stick insect loves me a bit.
When it gets to know me better
it will love me more
than my big sister loves her thick letter
from her special friend Mick,
or more than my mother loves her mother,
who is always sick, who watches the clock
go tick tock tick.

My stick insect climbs a green leaf
like the hand of a clock.
It has little bumps on its back
like a rickshaw on a bumpy road
and whiskers like my grandfather's,
although his are thick handlebars.
At night when the dark climbs downstairs
I watch my stick insect pick her way though my dreams.

THE WORLD OF TREES
(inspired by the Forest of Burnley)

Sycamore. Mountain ash. Beech. Birch. Oak.

In the middle of the forest the trees stood.
And the beech knew the birch was there,
and the mountain ash breathed the same air
as the sycamore, and everywhere

the wind blew, the trees understood each other:
how the river made the old oak lean to the east,
how the felled beech changed the currents of the wind,
how the two common ash formed a canopy

and grew in a complementary way.
Between them they shared a full head of hair.
Some amber curls of the one could easily
belong to the other: twin trees, so similar.

Sycamore. Mountain ash. Beech. Birch. Oak.

Some trees crouched in the forest, waiting
for another tree to die so they could
shoot up suddenly into that new space;
stretch out comfortably for the blue sky.

Some trees grew mysterious mushroom fungi –
shoelace, honey, intricate as a grandmother's lace.
The wind fluttered the leaves; the leaves flapped their wings;
birds flew from the trees. Sometimes they'd sing.

The tall trees, compassionate, understood everything:
grief – they stood stock-still, branches drooped in despair;
fear – they exposed their many roots, tugged their gold hair;
anger – they shook in the storm, pointed their bony fingers.

Sycamore. Mountain ash. Beech. Birch. Oak.

The trees knew each other's secrets
in the deep green heart of the forest.
Each tree loved another tree best.
Each tree, happy to rest, leaned a little to the east,

or to the west, when the moon loomed high above:
the big white eye of the woods.
And they stood together as one in the dark,
with the stars sparkling from their branches,

completely at ease, breathing in the cold night air,
swishing a little in the breeze,
dreaming of glossy spring leaves
in the fine, distinguished company of trees.

Sycamore. Mountain ash. Beech. Birch. Oak.

THE ROWANS

From the window of her sheltered house
the rowan tree collects its winter berries
on the tips of its long fingers.

The morning light lifts up its skirt
and moves slow as an old woman across the sky.
Mona MacFadden is up early as always,

her false teeth not yet in her mouth,
her hair net still on top of her head.
Two foam rollers sit expectant, waiting.

She bends down and turns the fire on.
Two bars for the day. Nippy out.
Skin on hands, papery thin.

But she's proud of her feet.
Nor a bunion or a callous on them.
Soft, like baby's skin.

Outside, she can hear the noises of the rowans:
fierce whispers of old women in the winter wind,
the determined chirp of the robin.

She dresses slowly – purple cardigan
for a bitter day – then, suddenly,
spots the red robin on the rowan tree,

all puffed out with its gloriously red chest.
She watches the bird, avid.
She loves the robin more than her husband.

She feeds the robin some fat from her ham.
It eats – peck, peck, peck pernickety –
like she eats her slice of tongue, two veg.

And then the night comes down on the rowans
and everywhere, full of the trust of light,
small lights behind closed curtains.

Later, every light is out.
The rowans are silent.
The old people toss and stutter, call out

the names of loved ones long gone.
The wily moon chases the clouds
through the sky like a young thing.

And the bright stars sing.

GREAT-GRANDMOTHER'S LAMENT

I used to think that children loved to see their granny.
I don't know what it is. I stand at the windae.
I've never had them running intae see me.
They are no here for mair than two minutes
and then they're running away from me, bony hands,
like I'm a bad auld witch spitting oot curses.
In then oot and I'm lucky if I get a chance to press
a pound into their hand; then it's up – off – away.
Nobody says *hooray!* Nobody bothers her shirt about me.
They're that gled to see the back of me:
round shoulders, hunched old woman, sticky-oot back.
Naebody's got a minute fir their granny.
If they would jist say, 'Granny, you'll never guess what?'
it would make their old granny so happy.
But you never get to hear onything; it's all whispers.
I huv tae say, 'What's she saying?' because she
sits there, little madam, and mumbles and mutters,

and I canny understand a word, and she's moody.
My great-grandchildren get served hand and foot
and here's me still cooking for myself –
my wee bit of veg, boiled ham. Nobody bothers
staying for longer than a pound coin sucked intae a wee fist.
I'm telling you. I'm not kidding you on.
It's no like the past for grannies these days:
nobody brings their granny a wee sweetie, a hazelnut toffee,
or sips their granny's sugary tea.
Everybody is that busy behind the TV screens;
nobody knows how to make a conversation
let alone make a home-made meal or a fresh baked scone.
I'm not kidding you on. They're good for nothing.
Oh, we're the poorer for it, the hale human race.
I'll tell you, I'll be gled tae get shot o' this place.

SHETLAND

Some men fall in love with a woman,
some women fall in love with a man,
some men fall in love with another man,
some women fall in love with another woman –
but I, my dear one, fell in love with Shetland.

The first time ever I saw her face,
the light on the land filled me with ease
and I knew I felt at home here
with the sea around me everywhere,
the lovely lilt of the oystercatcher.

I knew I'd have to come back here,
pack my bags and change my life,
settle down, buy a small croft in
Yell or Fetlar or North Roe,
Bressay or Whalsay or Hamnavoe.

I can't tell what makes the heart race –
the people, the talk, the light, the birds –
all I know is Shetland cast her spell,
worked her magic and pulled me in.
Now, take a look at my face, listen to my pledge.

I will never fall in love again, Shetland.

OVERBOARD

When you look over the boat, my friend,
what do you think you'll see in the sea?
Are you looking for something real –
a porpoise, a whale, a dolphin, a seal?
Or are you looking to see if the sea
reflects how you really feel?

When you look over the boat, my friend,
into the dark and stormy waters,
are you thinking about a lost father and son
who went out one morning and never returned,
or of the things that can't be undone,
or of the days you've spent on your own?

When you look over the boat, my friend,
into the wild and stormy sea,
are you thinking of all the big journeys
across the Atlantic into Aberdeen,
and all the people you've been and seen,
away and back, back and away again?

When you look over the boat, my friend,
the waves in their wisdom *again* and *again*
will let you be you, will give you memories
and take them away as you stare into the sea.
Your face is dreamy; your thoughts far away.
How many times does a woman cross the sea

before she bides at home and calls it a day?

WAY DOWN BELOW IN THE STREETS OF PARIS

I spied a small lonely boy.
I was his beautiful red balloon,
from morning through to noon,

through to the silvery moon.
The boy held me tight.
I waited as he dreamed me at night,

waited for first light
when we would wander the streets together,
in any kind of weather –

me, floating like a feather.
Not lonely now, I am his shadow.
Not sad now, I am his echo.

Not bored now, I am his meadow.
I am not a play thing; his loyalty
pulls at my long heart string.

THE MOON AT KNOWLE HILL

The moon was married last night
and nobody saw,
dressed up in her ghostly dress
for the summer ball.

The stars shimmied in the sky
and danced a whirligig;
the moon vowed to be true
and lit up the corn rigs.

She kissed the dark lips of the sky
above the summer house,
she in her pale white dress
swooned across the vast sky.

The moon was married last night,
the beautiful belle of the ball,
and nobody saw her at all –
except a small girl in a navy dress

who witnessed it all.

THE NINE LIVES OF THE CAT MANDU

When I was born
I was a familiar,
a black cat, Satan's favourite form.

Next life – I was in a room
you couldn't swing a cat in.
Outside it was raining cats and dogs.

It was a small house in a mews.
Soon I was like a cat on hot bricks,
like a cat on a hot tin roof –

until I fell off and landed on my feet.
I was sleek, sly, mysterious.
I was the cat's pyjamas.

I set the cat among pigeons.
I let the cat out of the bag.
One night, playing cat and mouse,

I lost a life under a white car,
my own dead form lit up by cat's eyes.
I came back ginger with long whiskers.

I escaped a catalogue of catastrophes.
I had good lives. I was worshipped
in Ancient Egypt. I was a Siamese,

a Manx, a sphinx, a Persian, a Burmese.
I lived lives of exquisite ease –
until I had bad catarrh in Catalonia.

I purred a catechism, prayed for baptism,
but fell into a catatonic state. No cat nap –
I was kaput. Capisch? My final date.

FIRST AND FOREMOST

My good points:
I am fresh, novel,
the genuine article.
I am unprecedented.
From the word go,
a healthy ego;
I'm incomparable,
bold and original.
Never backwards
in coming forwards.
Never put
off to tomorrow
what I can do
today. I rise at dawn
with the cockerel.
I reap the first fruits.
I put my good foot first.

I also first foot.
I am phenomenal,
first among equals.
I took the first step.
I made the first move.
I always stand up
to be counted.
I don't run away
from the truth.
I get things first
hand; I come straight
to the point.
'Hold on, hold on,'
I say. 'First things first.'
To sum up:
I'm quite exceptional.

My bad points:
I am first
to fly off the handle.
I am selfish, callous,
cruel, ruthless.
I look after number one.
I put myself first.
My friends call me
Numero Uno.
It pains me, but doesn't stop
me pushing
to be first in the queue.
'Oh!' I say snootily.
'First come first served.'
I don't care for
other numbers.
Useless losers.
I travel first class.
I throw the first stone.

I am Premier.
I am the first in my field.
I show off at first nights.
I believe in yours truly;
the first stroke
is half the battle.
Let's face things
frankly – I am the one
and only.

DOUBLE TROUBLE

We were rich and poor.
We were bought and sold.

We were black and white.
We were young and old.

We were life and death.
We were north and south.

We were hand in hand.
We were foot and mouth.

We were good and bad.
We were war and peace.

We were day and night.
We were man and beast.

We were hunger and greed.
We were water and land.

We were empty and full.
We were lost and found.

We had two strings to our bow.
We were in it together.

We were the spitting image.
We were the doppelganger.

We were terrible twins.
We were happy and sad.

We were alter ego.
We were sane and mad.

We were two-faced.
We were two-a-penny.

We spat, 'Double or quits.'
We sneered, 'Double the money.'

We liked to two-time.
We stayed in a twin-town.

We led a double life.
We lived in a two-up-two-down.

We were too much.
We were entwined.

We were a right pair.
We were in two minds.

We peered through bifocals.
We talked in double entendres.

We walked double-quick.
We never wandered.

We were a double act.
We were Morecambe and Wise.

We were Laurel and Hardy.
We were Jekyll and Hyde.

We were Romeo and Juliet.
We were tragedy and comedy.

We spoke tête-à-tête.
We were a carbon copy.

We dreamt in a double bed.
We were fluently bilingual.

We were in two minds.
We were never single.

We drove on dual carriageways.
We insisted on equal pay.

We were twinned; we were mated.
We loved and we hated.

We could not be separated.
We could not be separated.

SOUR SIXTEEN

Sweet sixteen I've never been.

I banged my bedroom door.
I snarled at my mother.
I loathed her.
I hated to be seen with her.
I hated my acne.
I despised my own company.
I was bitter. Acid.
I was tart. Livid.

Sweet sixteen I've never been.

I made sarcastic remarks.
I said, 'Get a life!'
I said, 'In your dreams!'
Nothing is what it seems.

Hairs grew under my arms.
My mother moaned,
'It's your hormones!'
I groaned, 'Hormones? You moron.'

Sweet sixteen I've never been.

My mother told me
my mates were unsavoury,
my tongue acerbic.
My mother screamed, frantic,
'You've turned sour!
Where's my lovely daughter?'
I said, 'Grown up. What's up?
Where've you been?'

Sweet sixteen I've never been.

FIRST X

I'll never forget
the first time –
that massive kiss.
It was past eight.
I was eighteen.
It was raining.
I worried I was late.
Rushed out of work,
nervy and anxious.
My hands shook.
It was momentous.
My palms sweated.
I trembled. I bit my lip.
At the last minute,
I worried about my choice.
I was secretive.
I made sure nobody saw.

Then, ever so carefully
I drew my kiss, checked
the right box, a bag of nerves.
Crossed my fingers for my candidate.
It was nearly polling time.
Past eight. I was nearly late.
I felt empathy with the suffragettes.
I whispered one name
all the way home:
Emmeline Pankhurst, under the stars,
under the equal light of the moon,
Emmeline Pankhurst, know this –
I have drawn my first cross.
Cheers, XXX

SURVEILLANCE

Maybe you are watching me, but then maybe
I am not who I say I am.
And when I leave my house and shut the door
and head for the station
I know my minutes are being taken,
frame by frame, shot by shot.

You have the technology to see me 24/7
and yet not see me at all.
Looking backwards I am all blurred, uncertain
of the future; the past is the hazy moment captured.
Play me back slowly and tell me who
I am supposed to be.

VALENTINE

I like your dreamy eyes.
I like your strange stories.
I like your soft shy lips.
I like your daft wee ways.
I like your lovely hands.
I like your snort of a laugh.
I like your witty jokes.
I like your love of gossip.
I like your funny dance.
I like you saying my name.
I like your humble kindness.
I like your lack of shame.
I like you fine. I like you a lot.
Will you be my – you know what?

NEW WEATHER

And in the old days we talked about the weather,
And it seemed it was always inexplicable.
We marvelled at rain or storms or high winds,
at hail or thunder or sheet lightning.

It was God's language, the weather –
God's wrath or mirth or anger.
Never our doing. We never blew up our own storms.
These days temperatures are rising;

in Madcaplane, Alaska, houses pitch and lean
in all directions. Nothing is level any more.
One minute baking heat, the next rain,
the next a hurricane with its own name.

The sea swells across Antarctica.
The ice sheets melt, the trees topple.
These days we are too hot to handle –
nowhere to run, hide or take shelter.

In the new days, we talk about the weather.

GLOSSARY OF SHETLAND TERMS USED IN 'THE KNITTER'

hame will dae me – home will do me/home suits me fine

a yarn aye – yarn always; yarn is the wool, but it is also a word for a tall tale or a story

gravits – scarves or mufflers

lay on sweeric geng – finish the first row

takkin my makkin – bringing your work with you; makkin is what you are making, your knitting

een and een – one and one

NOTES AND ACKNOWLEDGEMENTS

Some of these poems have been commissioned by the Barbican Education Department, the Forest of Burnley, the National Theatre of Scotland, Theatre Cryptic and the Scottish Poetry Library. 'My Face is a Map' was inspired by talking to the scientist Iain Hutchinson, who runs Saving Faces, and commissioned by the Royal Society of Medicine. 'Surveillance' was commissioned by Performing Arts Lab for ESPRC and 'New Weather' was commissioned by the *Sunday Herald*. Some of the poems were published in *Number Party*.